ISBN – 978-1722160517

Matt Shaw Publications

www.mattshawpublications.co.uk

www.facebook.com/mattshawpublications

Colour My Cock

An Adult Colouring Book

Designed And Illustrated By

Matt Shaw

My name is Matt Shaw. I'm married with no children because, unlike my drawing pencils, my personal pencil contains no lead. I do not know this for a fact, it's just a guess. In my spare time, I have an unhealthy obsession with drawing dicks.

Some of you may be purchasing this book just because you fancy colouring in some dicks. Fair enough. You may have no idea who I am. For those of you in that position; I am the published author of over 200 books. I write in the horror genre mainly although I have also penned novels in other genres too. I have recently branched out into making films. In 2018, I completed my feature length horror *MONSTER*.

The other books - and projects - have very little to do with dicks.

Oh, tell a lie… I wrote and illustrated another book called *Mr. Prick And The Dirty Cunt*.

I regret nothing.

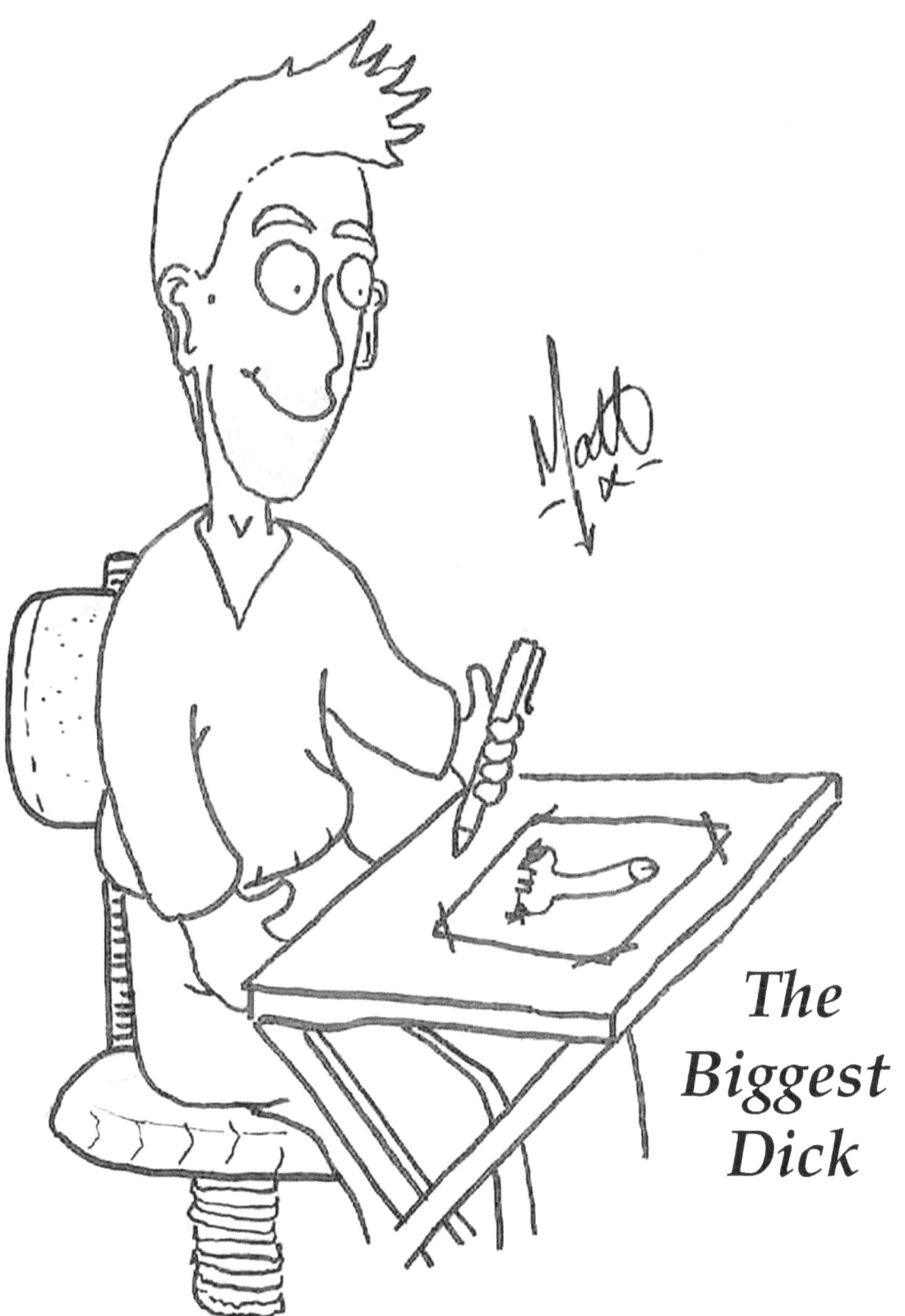

The Biggest Dick

The Spitting Cock

The spitting cock is a classic. I don't know many men who, at some point of their life, have not drawn one. I myself often draw one in books I am asked to sign. To be really fancy, I hide my signature amongst the ejaculate.

I once did a convention in America. A man came to the table and told me he wanted to buy a book. He had no idea who I was and fancied giving one a go. He said, 'I'll only buy it if you draw a cock in the book though.'

My response?

'Boy, have you come to the right table...'

The Spitting Cock

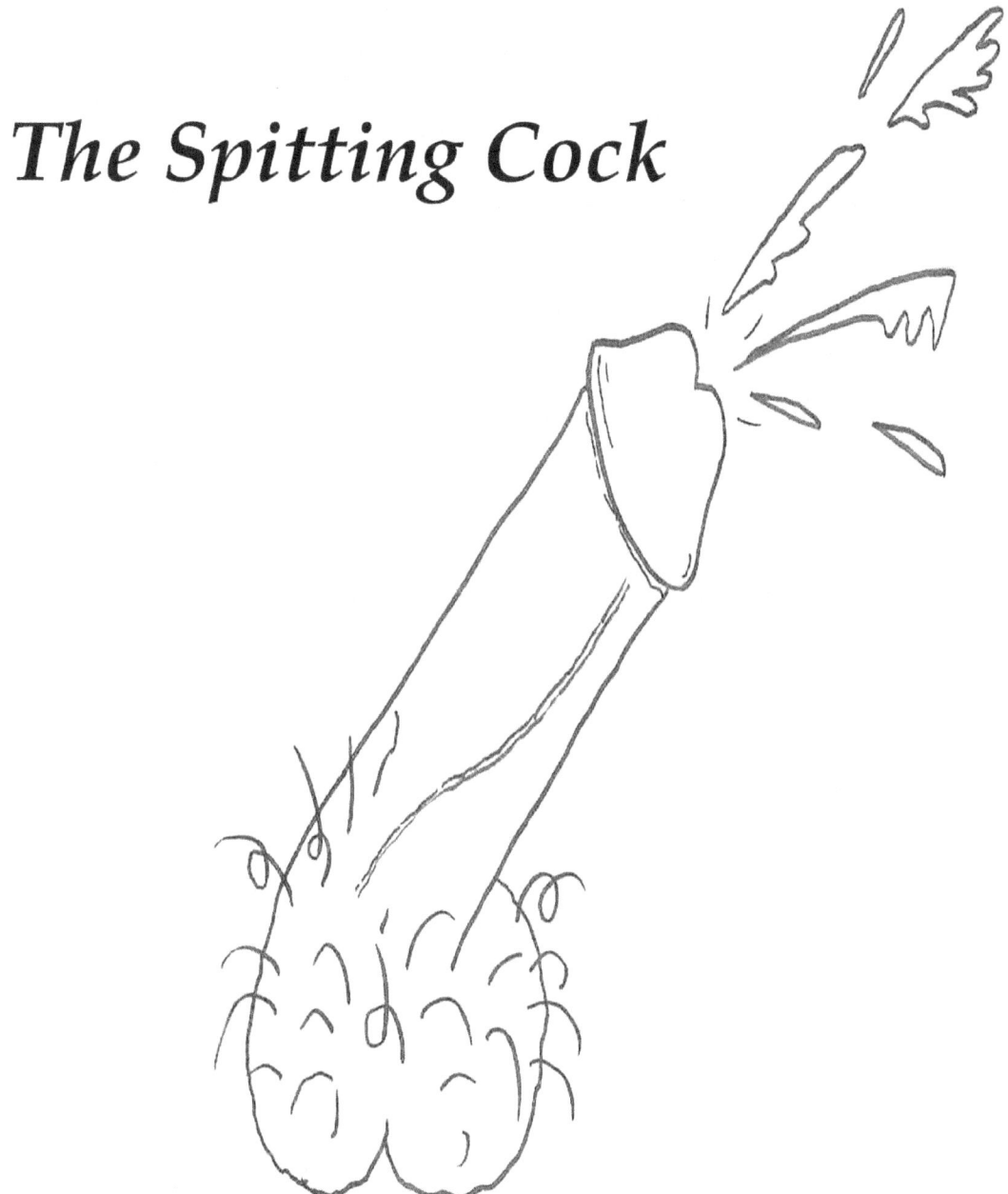

The Disappointment

Come on, people, you can't deny you haven't seen a few of these in your lifetime. You see the bulge in the pants and get excited at the thought of what you're about to receive. You unwrap the goods only to find - actually - it wasn't really worth unwrapping.

Much like Christmas presents from Grandparents in some respects. You see the gift beneath the tree, you get all excited, you tear into the wrapping and - oh - is that it?

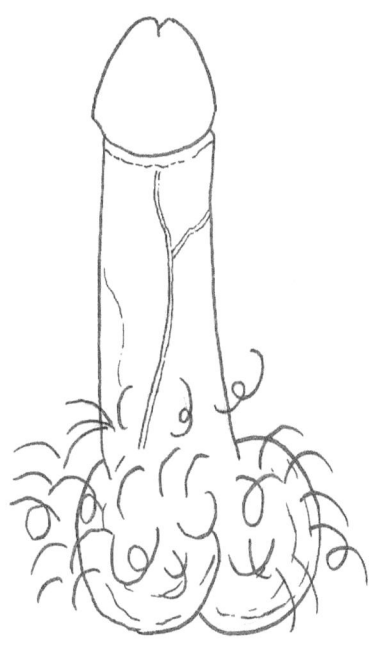

The Disappointment

The Matt Shaw

Form a queue, ladies, and prepare yourselves to discover that I used a lot of artistic licence in this particular drawing…

The Matt Shaw

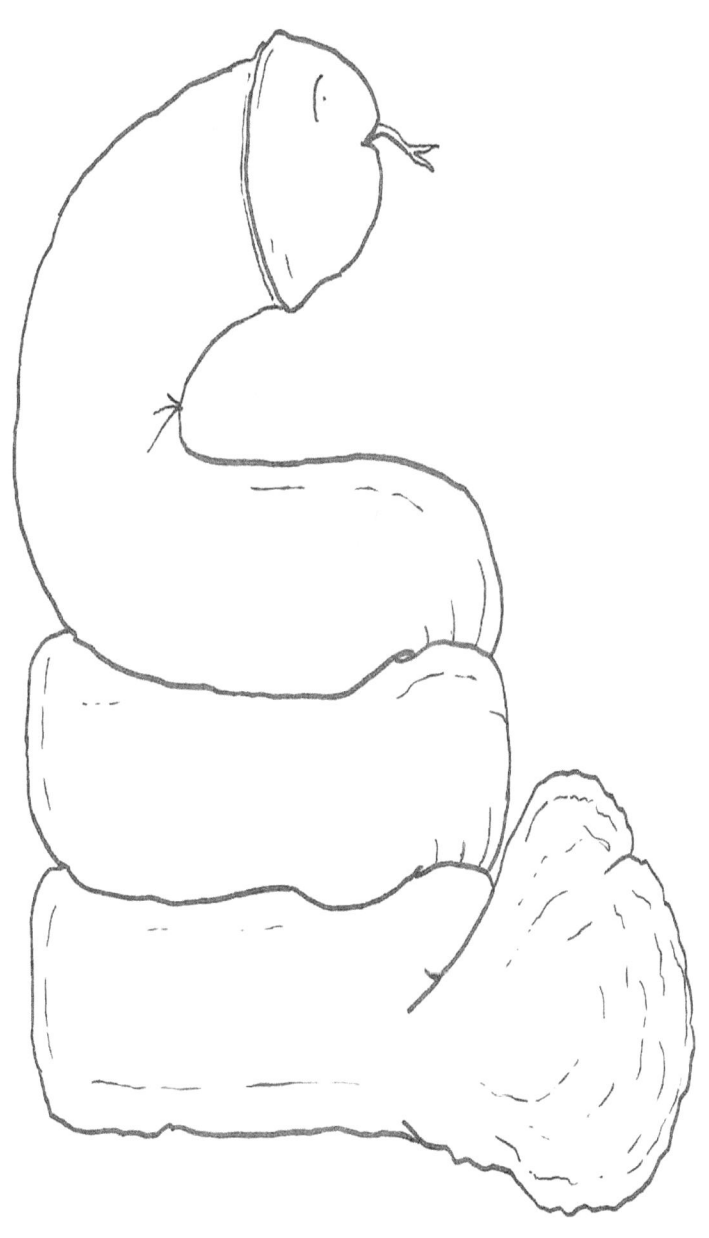

The Uncut

Now I was "cut" at a really young age. So young in fact that I only vaguely remember it (thank God). So, to get this right, I had to Google Image it.

Seeing all these dicks with their foreskin kind of makes me thankful for mine being cut, even if they did take a little too much off the top.

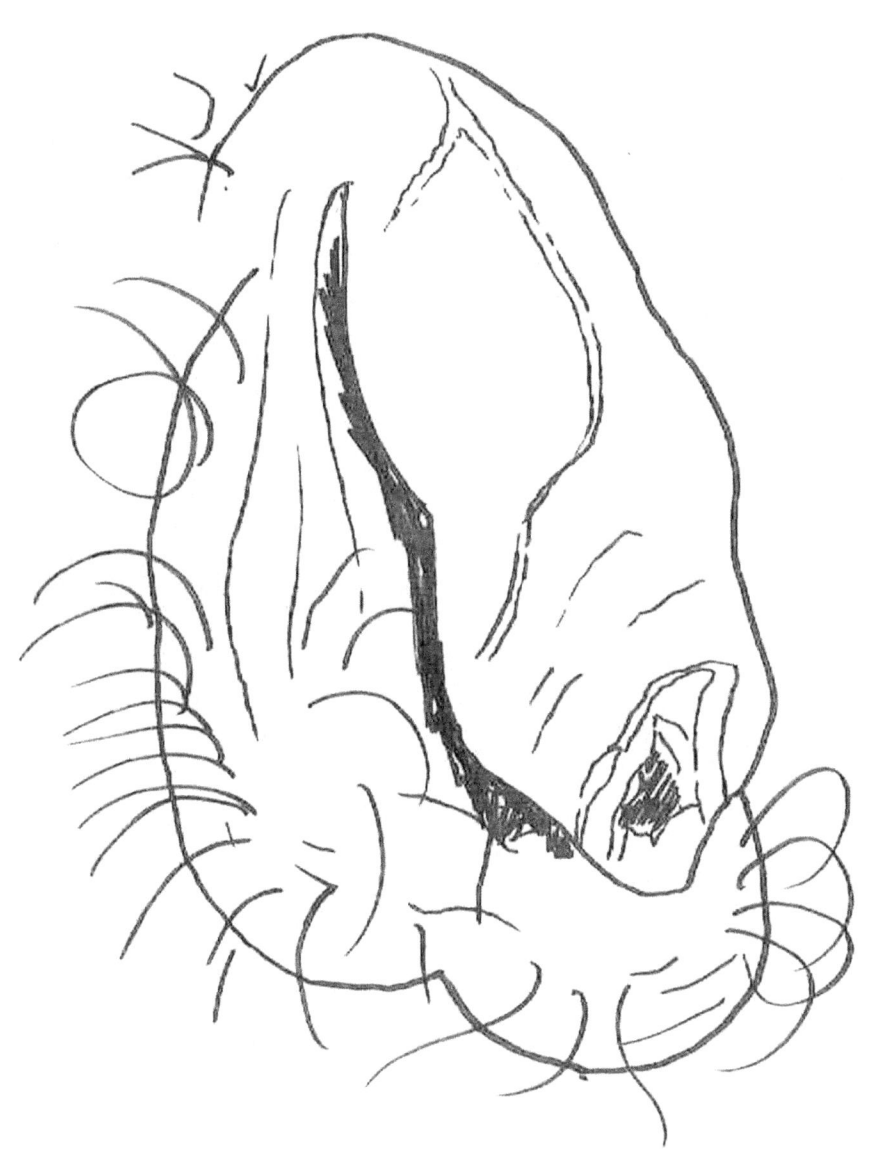

The
Uncut

Where's Willy?

So - who fancies a game?

Personally I prefer the game "Let's Hide Willy". I have hidden my willy in loads of places over the years... I've hidden it in vaginas, mouths, assholes, between cushions, various sex toys and - most likely - your mum.

Where's Willy?

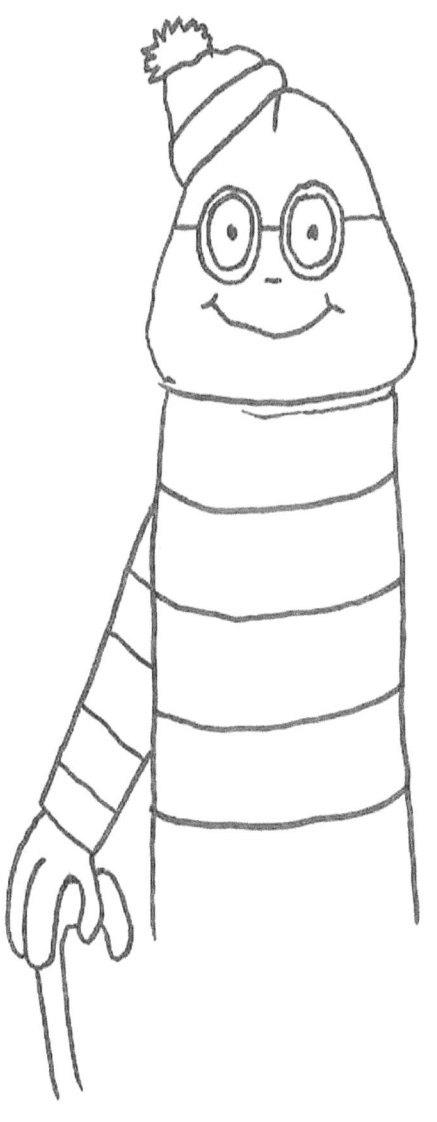

The Drowned Dick

It might not look very pretty once you've finished the task in hand but - by Jove - it's better than the alternative.

When you have sex, you want an orgasm… You don't want any added surprises…

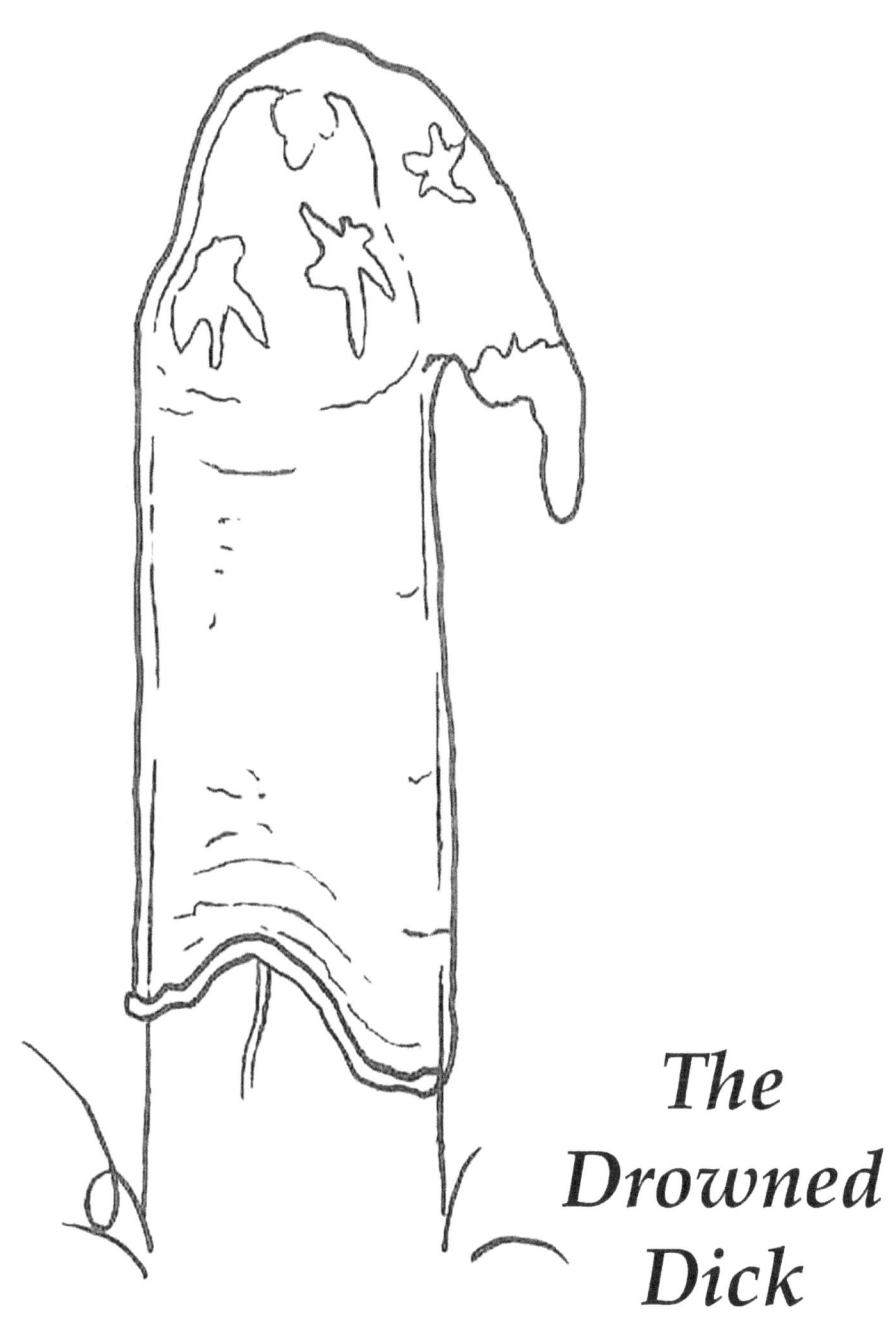

The
Drowned
Dick

The Dirty Dick

Speaking of hidden surprises from one-night stands… Here's an example:

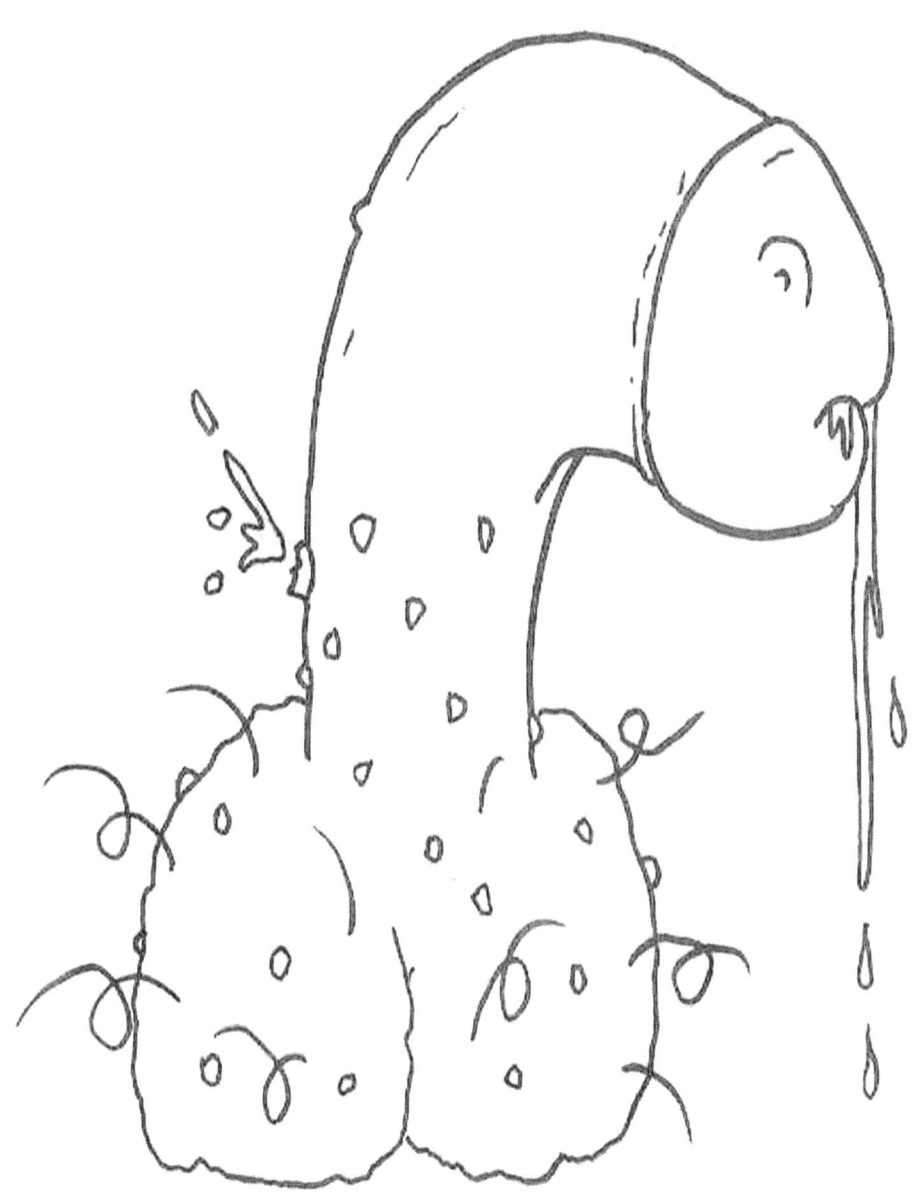

The Dirty Dick

The Cheat

Consider this one a warning.

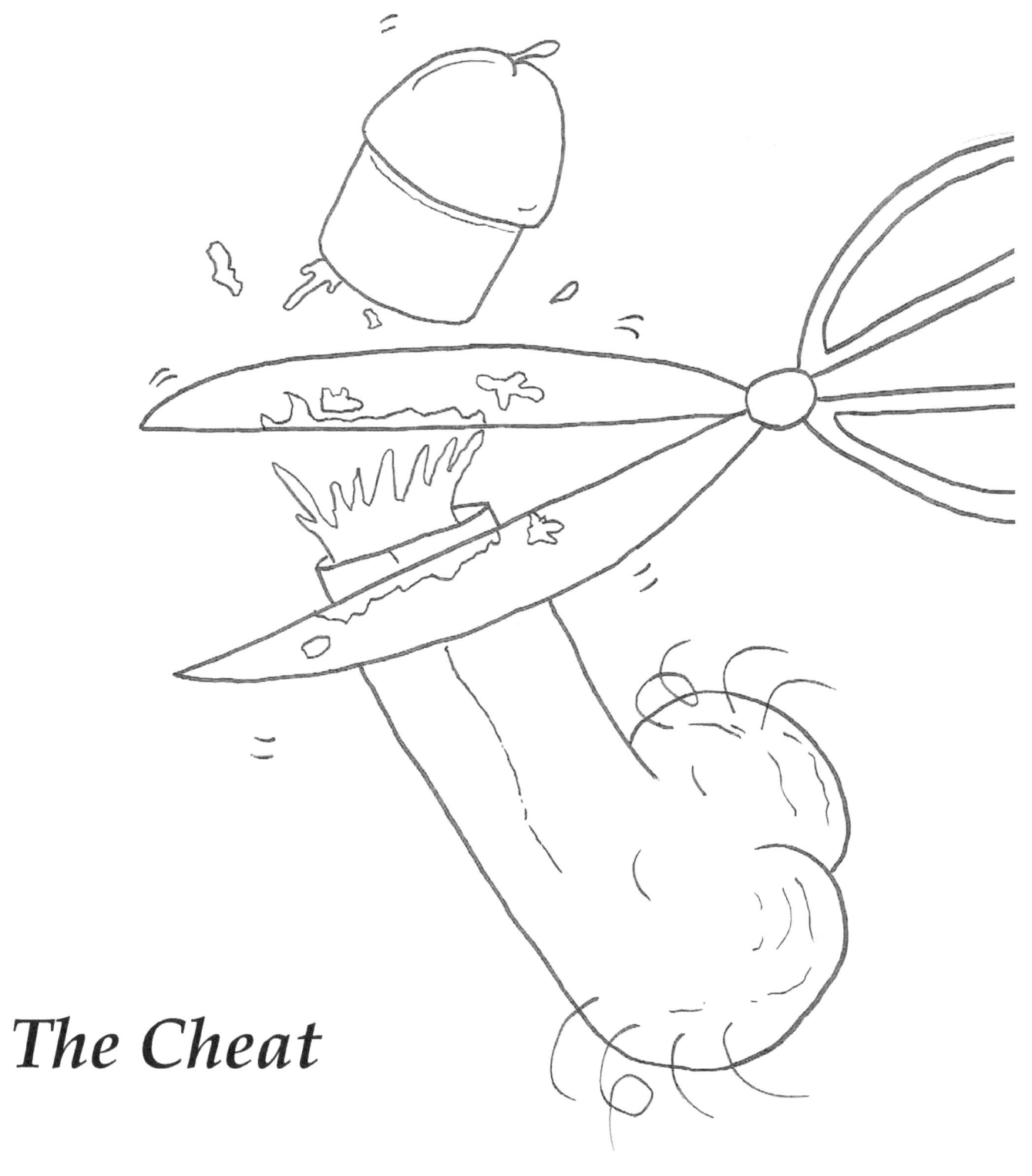

The Cheat

The Premature Dick

In keeping with The Disappointing Dick.

Tip for the men: When going on a date, have a wank before you go. That way, if you get lucky, you're not going in with a loaded gun. Although, if I need to tell you this, there's no helping you anyway. It's common sense and if you don't already unload first, you clearly have none.

The Premature Dick

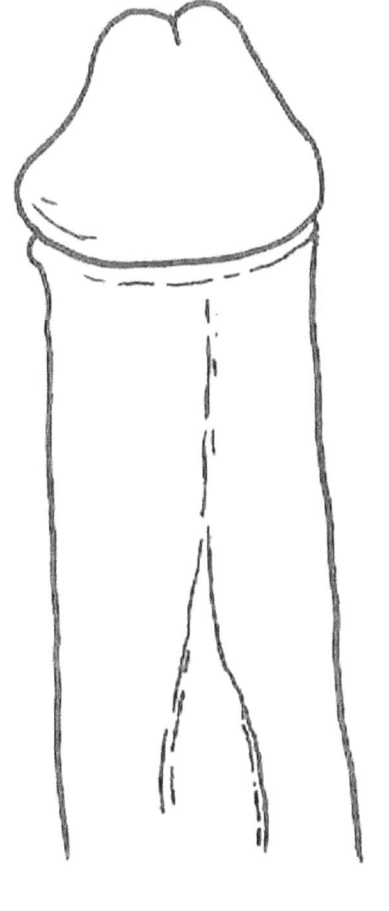

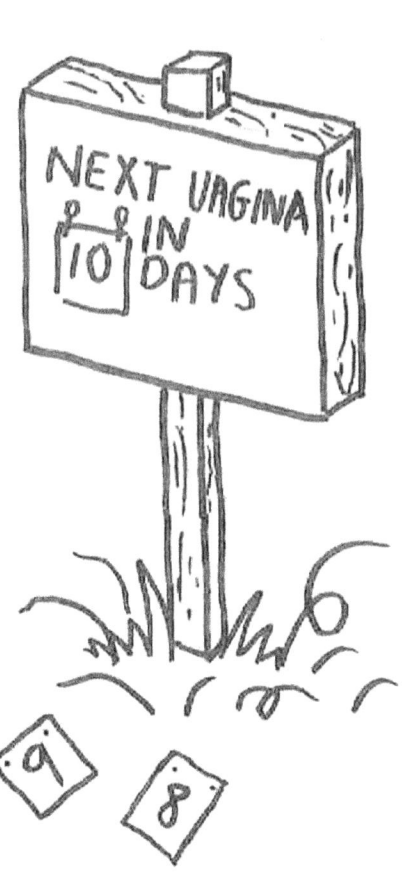

The Explosive Orgasm

Sometimes it is good to go without for a few hours (what can I say? I'm a wanker). That way, when you next blow your load… You *literally* blow it…

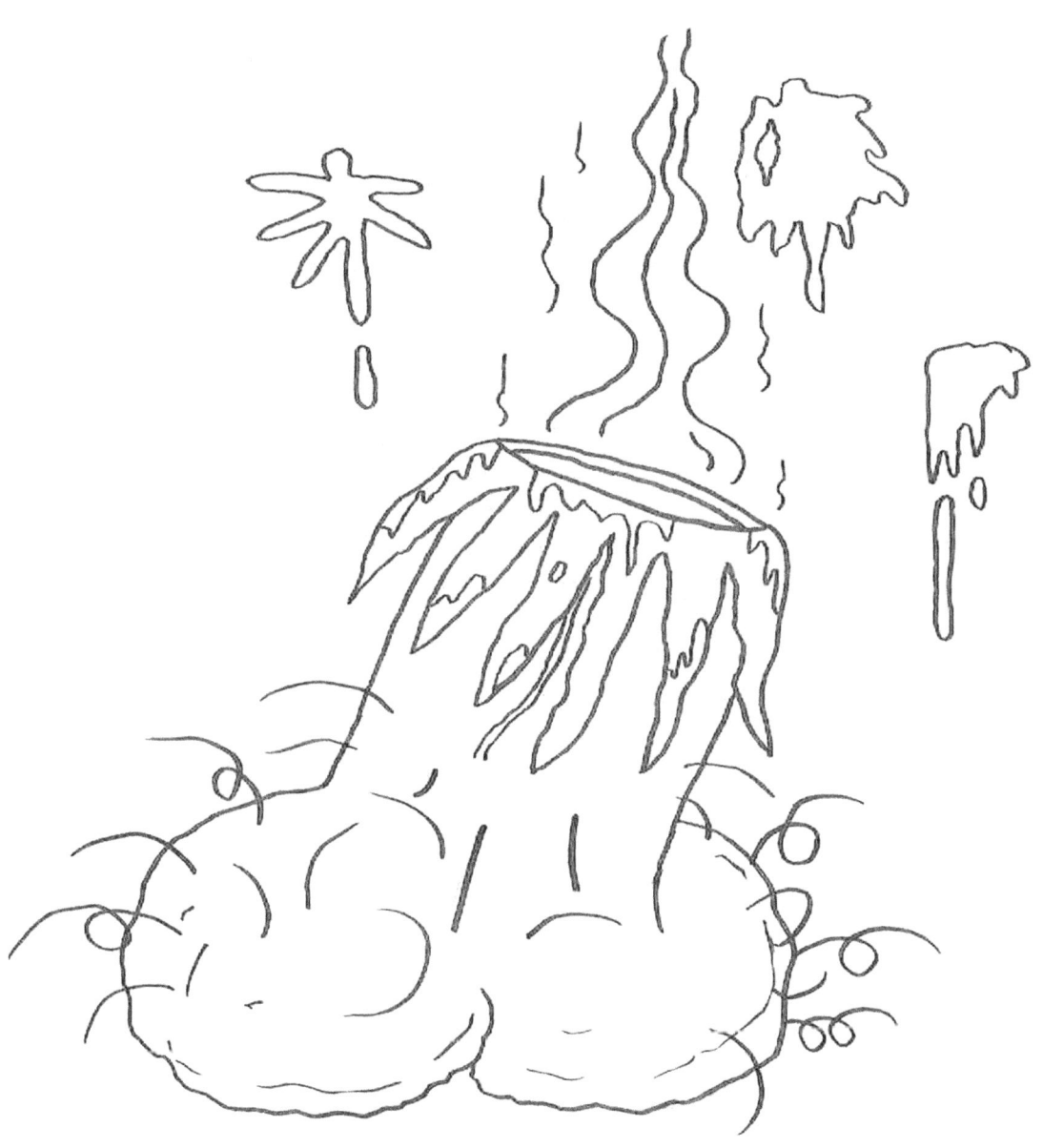

The Explosive Orgasm

The Post-Op Dick

We are not here to judge people. We are here to colour.

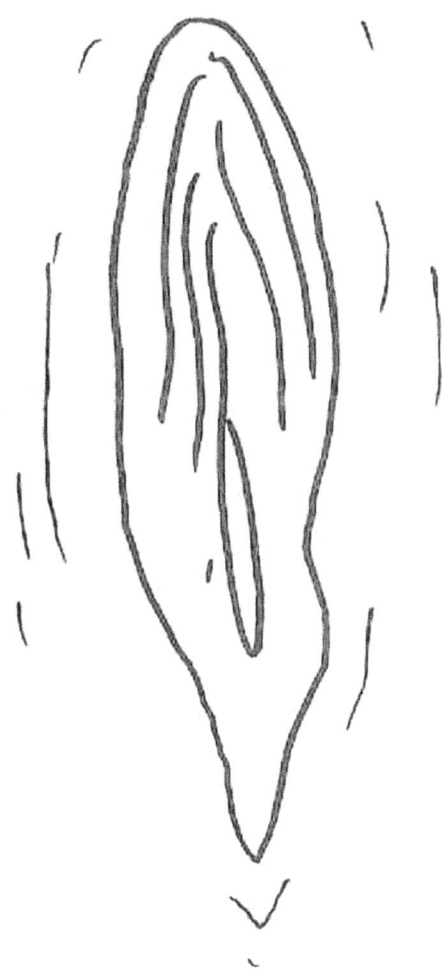

The Post-Op Dick

The Stick-Man's Erection

A little time out. Instead of colouring, why not try and draw the rest of the stick-man? Really let loose with your artistic skills.

The Stick-Man's Erection

The Dick Van Dyke

Come on, we all knew this was a *necessity*.

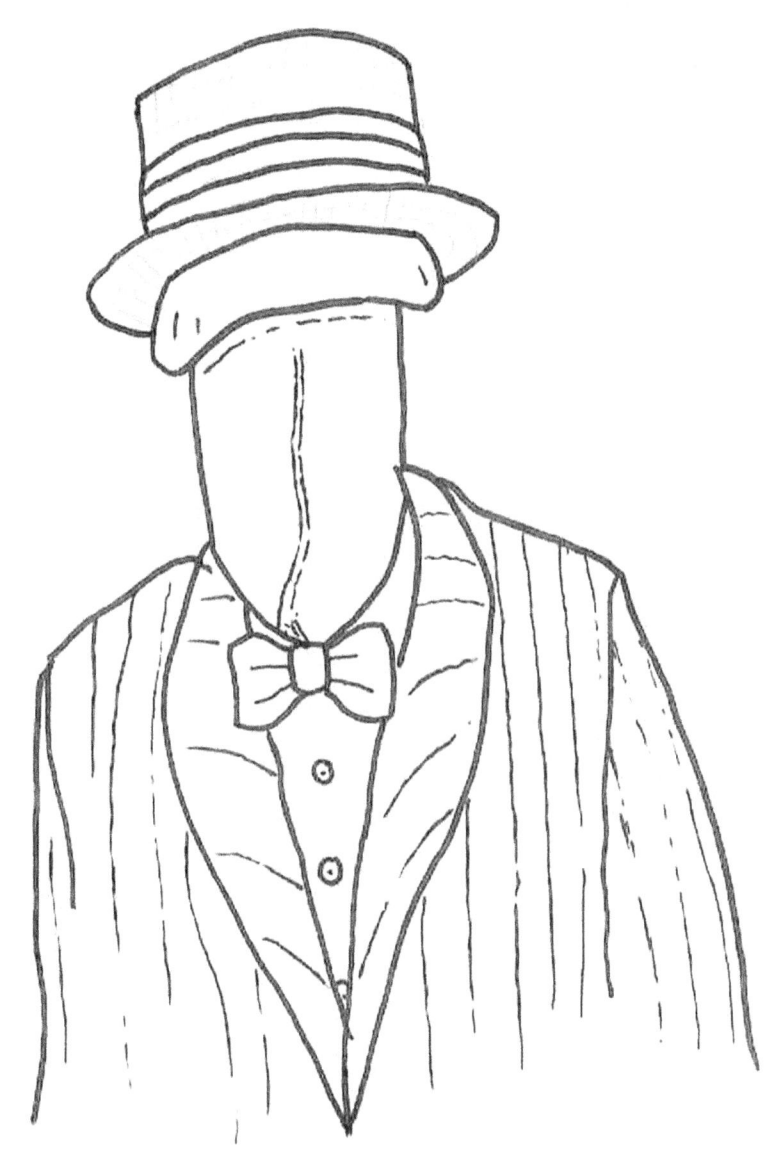

The Dick Van Dyke

The Strike It Lucky

Ah the old matchstick dick. Thankfully I don't quite have this type of penis but I am not far off. I feel sorry for men who cocks like this. I just hope they learned how to use their tongue…

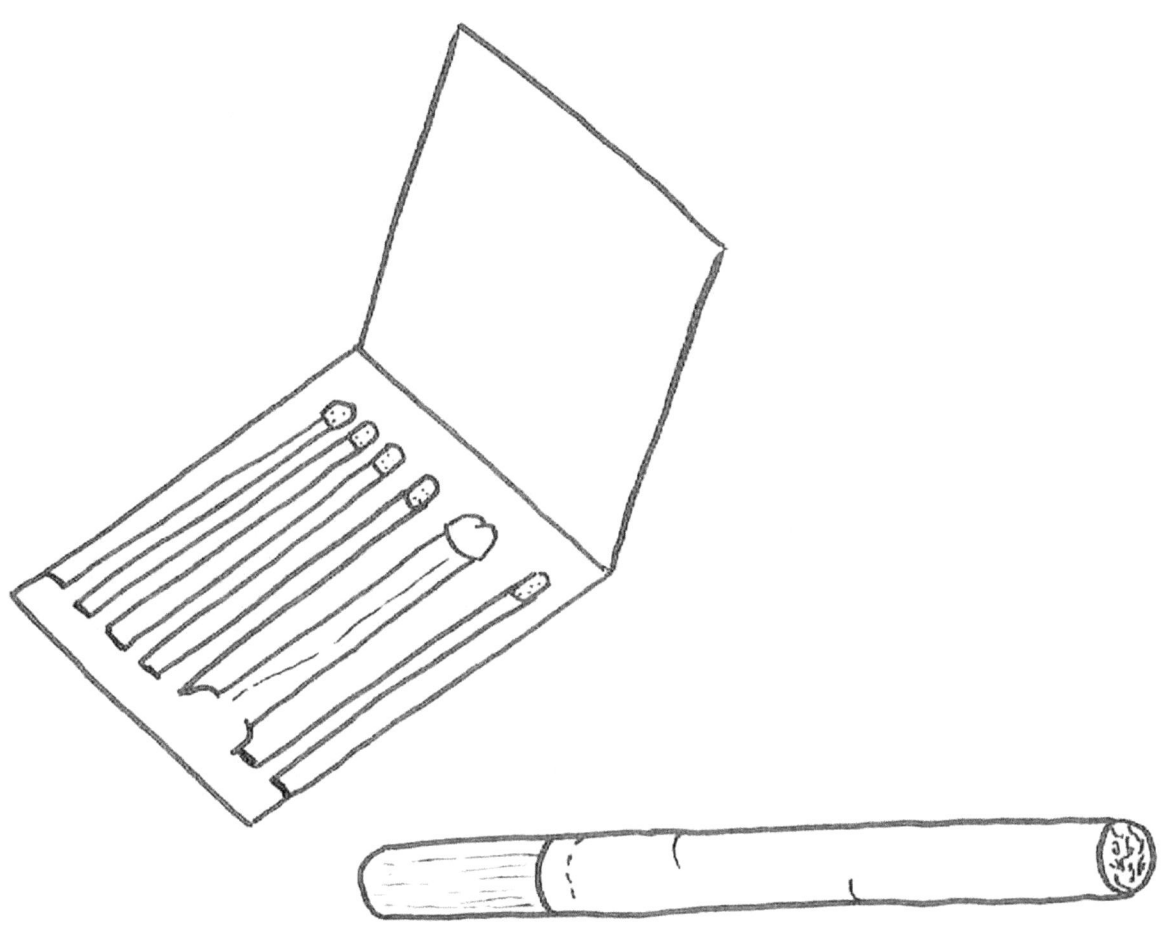

Strike It Lucky

The Cocky Cock

All men wish we had one of these but - most of the time - we just blindly stab away with our pricks until we get lucky and find the right hole (or the wrong hole, on special occasions).

Speaking of special occasions... Publishing a book is a special occasion.

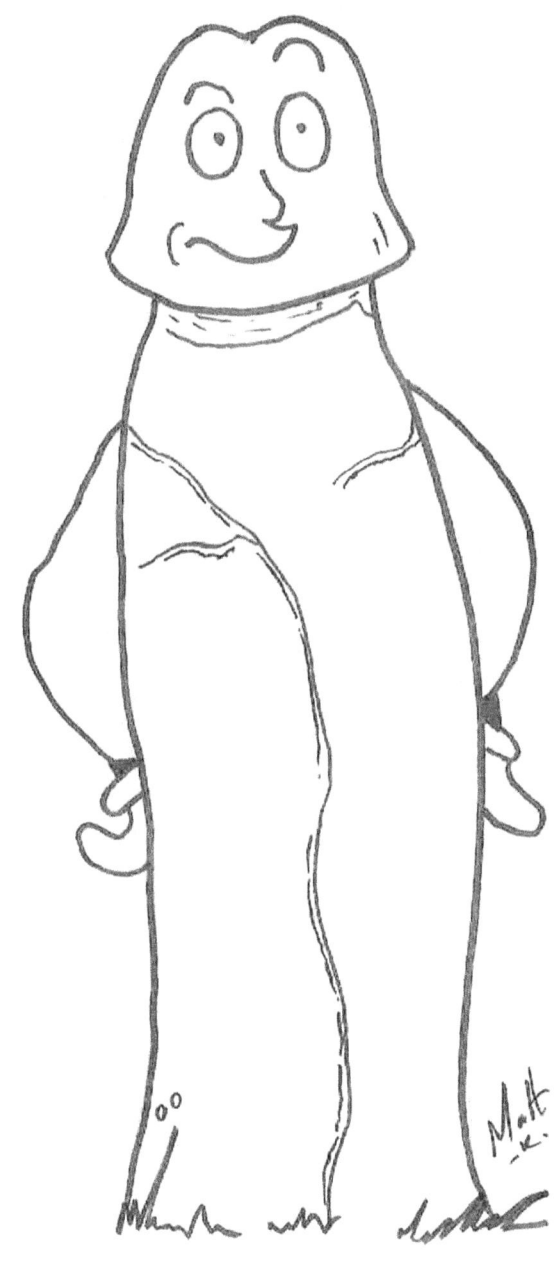

The Cocky Cock

A Different Dick

Nope. I just cannot bring myself to do it. I mean, if someone offered me a lot of money I would but - no way. Apparently, those who have done this have said, it really hurts when you have your first wee-wee.

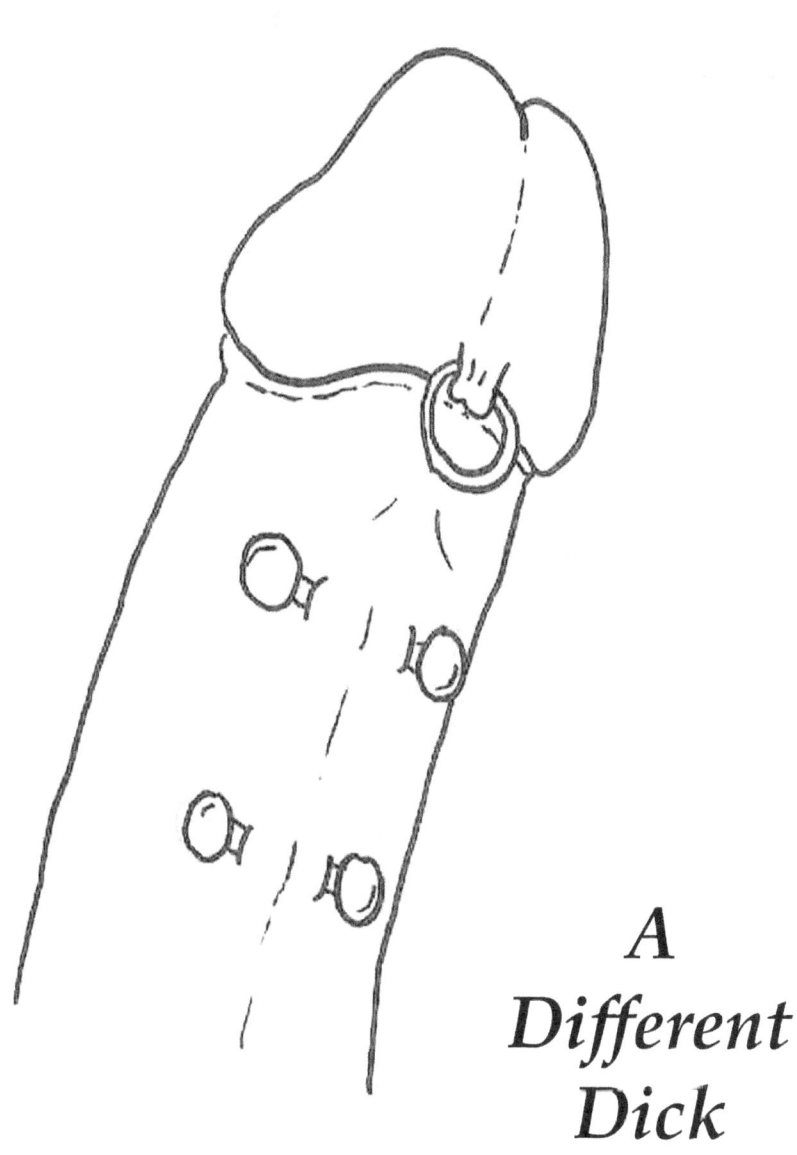

A
Different
Dick

The Pencil Dick

One step up from matchstick dick.

For those curious: I fall somewhere between the two.

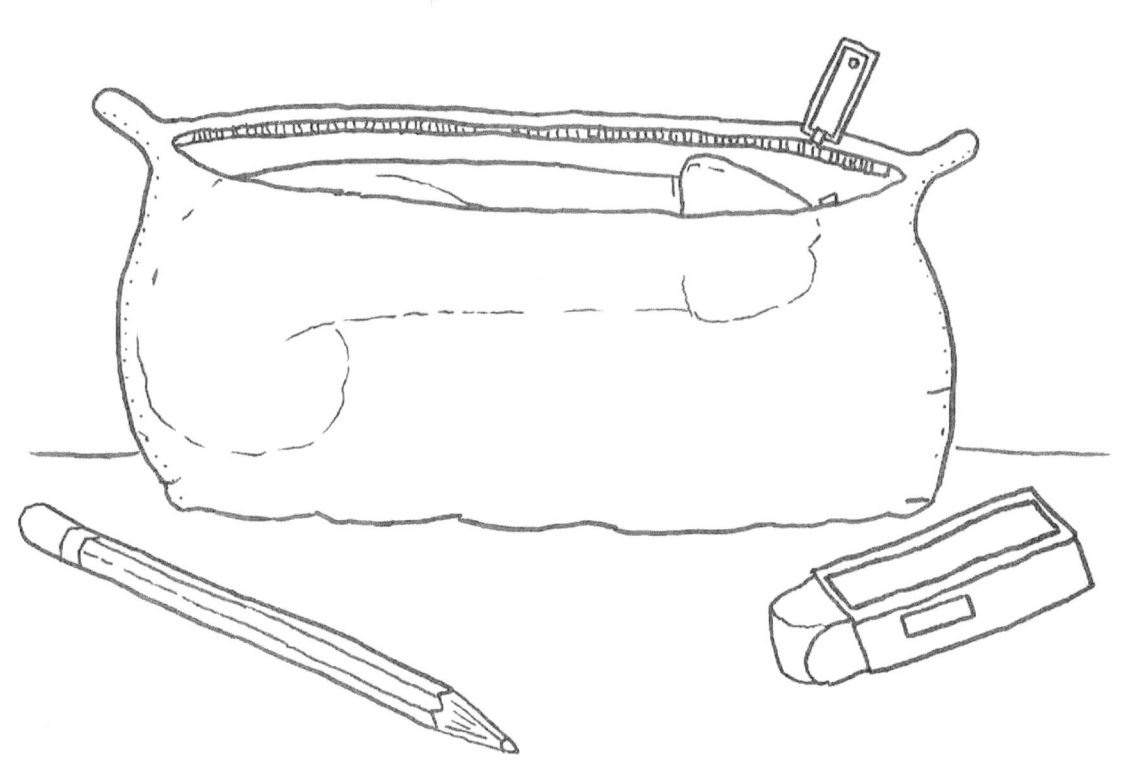

The Pencil Dick

The "I'm Experimenting" Dick

Don't knock it until you have tried it. Men have a special sweet-spot in their butts. Stroke that right and... See the "explosive orgasm" picture.

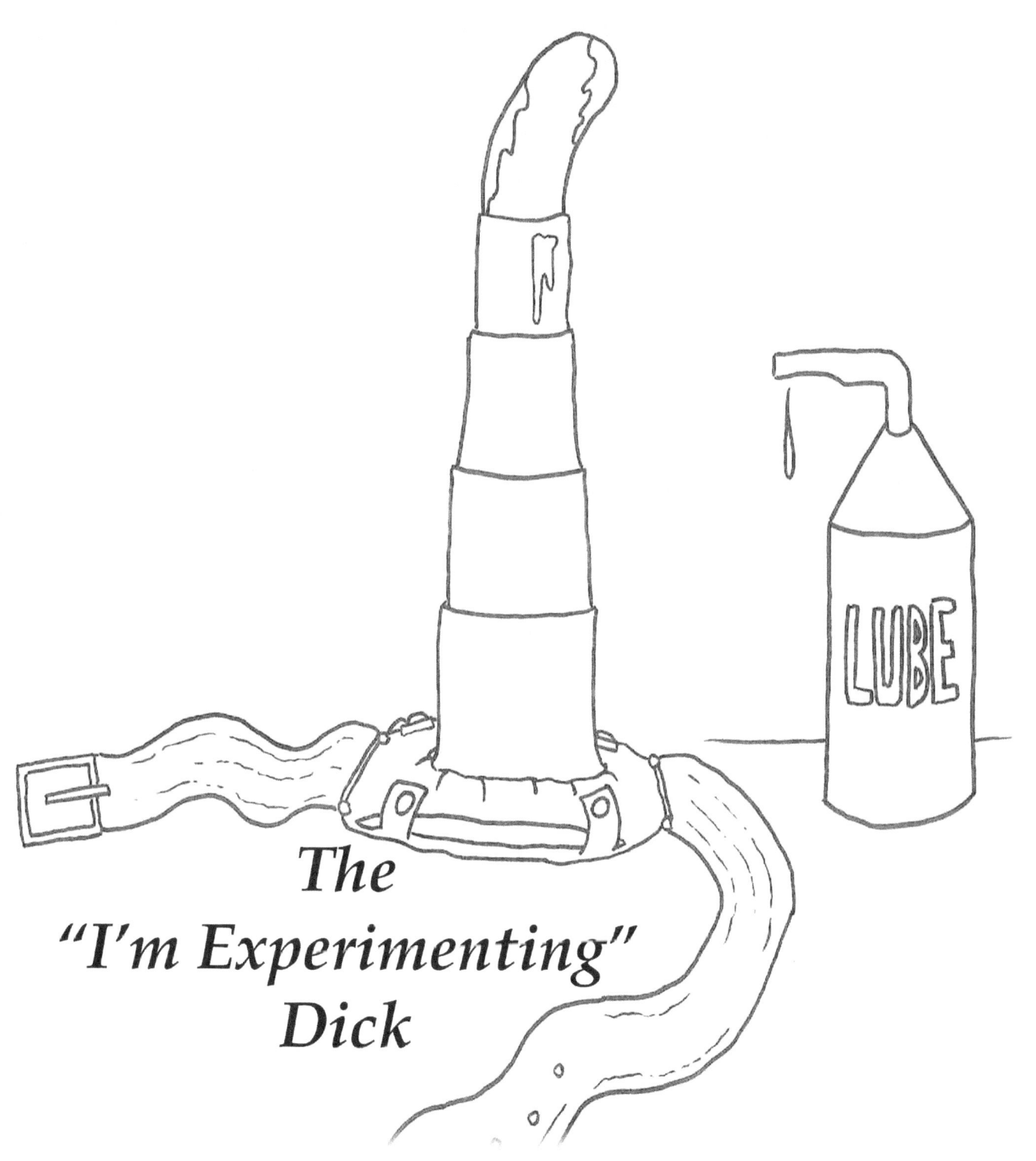

The
"I'm Experimenting"
Dick

And there we have it… A book of dicks to colour in.

Maybe you got bored and thought of better dicks to draw than the ones within this collection? Well - you know what you need? A notepad to make notes of such things to draw…

Available on Amazon

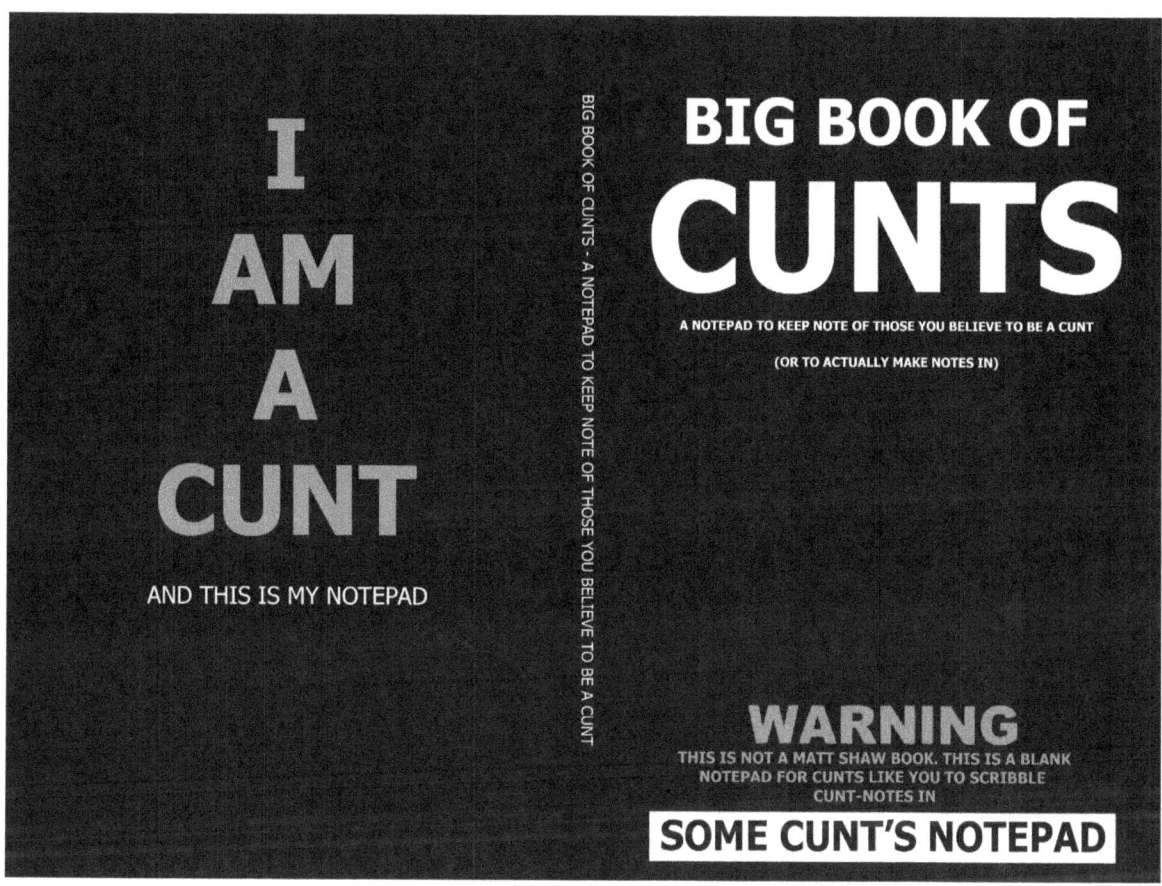